Animal World

Animal Patterns

Patricia Whitehouse

Raintree

www.raintreepublishers.co.uk
Visit our website to find out more information about **Raintree** books.

To order:
☎ Phone 44 (0) 1865 888112
▤ Send a fax to 44 (0) 1865 314091
💻 Visit the Raintree Bookshop at **raintreepublishers.co.uk** to browse our catalogue and order online.

First published in Great Britain by Raintree, Halley Court, Jordan Hill, Oxford OX2 8EJ, part of Harcourt Education.
Raintree is a registered trademark of Harcourt Education Ltd.

Editorial: Nick Hunter and Diyan Leake
Design: Sue Emerson (HL-US) and Michelle Lisseter
Picture Research: Amor Montes de Oca (HL-US) and Maria Joannou
Production: Lorraine Hicks

Originated by Dot Gradations
Printed and bound in China by South China Printing Company

ISBN 978 1 844 21537 9 (hardback)
07 06 05 04 03
10 9 8 7 6 5 4 3 2 1

ISBN 978 1 844 21542 3 (paperback)
11 10 09
10 9 8 7 6 5 4 3 2

British Library Cataloguing in Publication Data
Whitehouse, Patricia
Animal Patterns
516.1'5
A full catalogue record for this book is available from the British Library.

Acknowledgements
The publishers would like to thank the following for permission to reproduce photographs: Alan Paterson p. 4; Cathy and Gordon ILLG pp. 22, 24; Cincinnati Zoo/Ron Austing p. 13, back cover (cheetah); Corbis pp. 5 (Frank Lane Picture Agency), 11 (W. Wayne Lockwood, M.D.), 18 (Kennan Ward), 19 (Papilio), back cover (toucan, Frank Lane Picture Agency); Eda Rogers p. 9; FLPA p. 23 (Winifred Wisniewski); Paul Souders pp. 16, 17; PhotoDisc pp. 6, 8, 10, 12; Stock Photography pp. 14 (Jim Gray), 15 (Jim Gray), 20 (Anthony Mercieca/ Photophile), 21 (Anthony Mercieca/Photophile); Tom Stack & Associates p. 7 (Mark Allen Stack)

Cover photograph of zebra pattern, reproduced with permission of PhotoDisc

Every effort has been made to contact copyright holders of any material reproduced in this book. Any omissions will be rectified in subsequent printings if notice is given to the publishers.

Contents

What makes a pattern?

Patterns are shapes and colours that repeat.

This zebra crossing is a pattern on the road.

There are patterns on animals, too.

This toucan has stripes on its beak.

What pattern does a zebra have?

This is the pattern on a zebra.

It has black and white stripes.

A zebra looks like a horse with stripes.

What pattern does a tiger have?

This is the pattern on a tiger.

It has black stripes on its gold hair.

A tiger looks like a big cat
with stripes.

What pattern does a giraffe have?

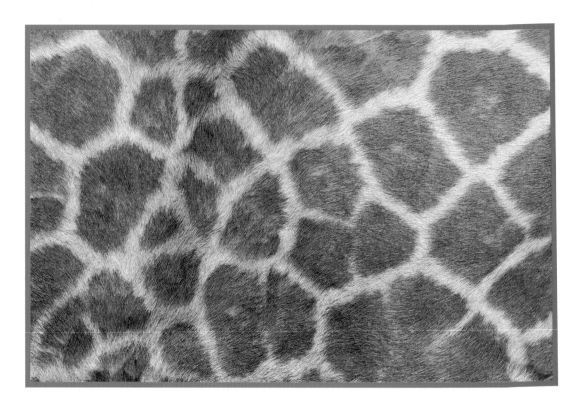

This is the pattern on a giraffe.

It has dark brown spots on light brown fur.

The spots go all the way up the giraffe's long neck.

What pattern does a cheetah have?

This is the pattern on a cheetah.

It has black spots on its yellow fur.

A cheetah looks like a big spotted cat.

What pattern does a jaguar have?

This is the pattern on a jaguar.

It has black circles on light brown fur.

A jaguar looks like a big cat with a circle pattern on it.

What pattern does a hyena have?

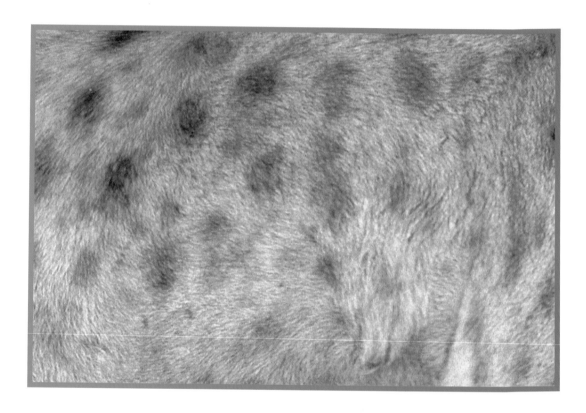

This is the pattern on a hyena.

It has brown spots on its brown fur.

A hyena looks a bit like a spotted dog.

What pattern does a gila monster have?

This is the pattern on a gila monster.

(We say, *heela monster.*)

A gila monster has spots and stripes.

It has spots on its back and stripes on its tail.

What pattern does a rattlesnake have?

This is the pattern on a rattlesnake.

It has diamond shapes on its skin.

The pattern goes from its head
to its tail.

What pattern does a peacock have?

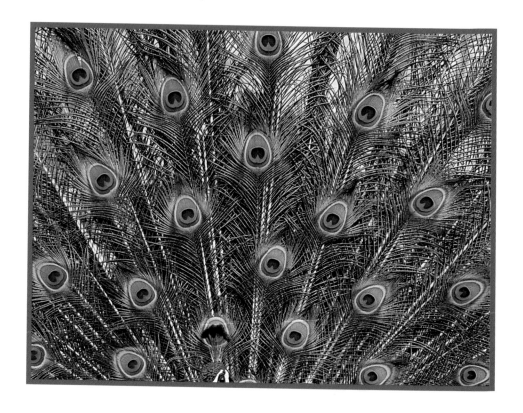

This is the pattern on a peacock's tail.

The pattern looks like lots of eyes.

A peacock can show off its
great big tail.

Index